RECALIBRATE

Adopting and Adapting to a New Generation in Your Workforce

RECALIBRATE

Adopting and Adapting to a New Generation in Your Workforce

TONY JEARY
The RESULTS Guy™

MIKE MCDANIEL
Leadership Architect™

RESULTS FASTER!
PUBLISHING

ISBN: 978-1-956370-70-6

© 2025 Tony Jeary & Michael McDaniel

All rights reserved. No part of this book may be reproduced, stored in a retrieval system, or transmitted, in any form or by any means, electronic, mechanical, photocopying, recording, or otherwise, without the prior written permission of the copyright holder, except for brief quotations embodied in critical reviews and certain other non-commercial uses permitted by copyright law.

Published by RESULTS Faster! Publishing
2591 Lakeside Parkway, Suite #200, Flower Mound, TX 75022

Printed in the United States of America

Disclaimer: The information provided in this book is for general informational purposes only. Readers are encouraged to seek professional advice before making any business decisions.

CONTENTS

INTRODUCTION: NAVIGATING THE NEW WORKFORCE MINDSET	XI
THE EMERGENCE OF A NEW WORKFORCE	XIII
ADAPTING VS. ADOPTING	XV
THE CHANGING LANDSCAPE	XVII
HOW THIS BOOK CAN HELP	XVIII
PART ONE: WHY DOES IT MATTER?	**1**
CHAPTER ONE: THE POWER OF PERSPECTIVE	3
PRINCIPLES	3
DISTINCTIONS	6
CHAPTER TWO: THE ART OF ADOPTION	15
ROADBLOCKS AND RECALIBRATIONS	17
ADOPT OR ADAPT?	19
CHAPTER THREE: THE ART OF ADAPTATION	21
ROADBLOCKS TO ADAPTATION AND HOW TO SOLVE THEM	25

RECALIBRATE

ADAPT OR ADOPT?	28
CHAPTER FOUR: BALANCING TRADITION AND INNOVATION	31

PART TWO: HOW DO YOU RECALIBRATE? — 43

CHAPTER FIVE: EFFECTIVE COMMUNICATION	45
CHAPTER SIX: THE POWER OF ORGANIZATIONAL CULTURE	55
BRAND	55
COMMUNICATION	57
FAST PACED	58
HOW DO YOU RECALIBRATE?	59
TYING IT ALL TOGETHER	60
CHAPTER SEVEN: PROCESS-DRIVEN SUCCESS	63
THE COST OF ANTIQUATED SYSTEMS	63
ATTRACTING THE RIGHT TALENT WITH MODERN TOOLS	67
CHAPTER EIGHT: SOCIAL MEDIA AS A FORCE MULTIPLIER	71
SOCIAL MEDIA AS A TOOL FOR SCREENING	73
BUILDING AN INTERACTIVE SOCIAL MEDIA CULTURE	74

PART THREE: ACTION STEPS — 77

CHAPTER NINE: CLOSING THE BACK DOOR	79
INTENTIONALITY IN RETENTION	79
USING TECHNOLOGY TO STAY AHEAD OF ATTRITION	82

CONTENTS

CHAPTER TEN: ATTRACTING QUALITY TALENT	**85**
THE POWER OF REFERRALS	85
BEING A QUALITY COMPANY	86
MAKE IT EASY TO BE FOUND	87
PLAY NICE IN THE SANDBOX	87
CONCLUSION	**89**
ABOUT THE AUTHORS	**91**
WHAT WE CAN DO FOR YOU	**95**

INTRODUCTION: NAVIGATING THE NEW WORKFORCE MINDSET

In every leadership luncheon I attend, without fail, the same pressing question is brought up: **How do we navigate the new mindset of young people entering the workforce?** This question reflects a broader concern shared by managers and executives alike—how to effectively communicate with and get buy-in from a generation that approaches work and life differently from their predecessors.

In the past, managing a workforce involved clear, hierarchical structures and well-defined roles. The expectations were straightforward: show up on time, follow instructions, and work diligently. Many times, these roles were hard, metric driven, and managed with an expected sense of urgency. Motivators would range from promises of making a lot of money to fear of losing the job. Times have changed. Take, for example, my son-in-law. Unlike my generation, he isn't motivated by money. His primary goal isn't to earn millions or climb the corporate ladder. Instead, he seeks harmony in his life—a balance between work and personal time. He wants to enjoy going to work just as much as he enjoys going home at the end of the day. For him, peace of mind and a fulfilling life outweigh the financial rewards that might come with a high-stress, high-paying job.

RECALIBRATE

This shift in motivation is not unique to my son-in-law; it reflects a broader trend among younger workers. The traditional motivators—fear of unemployment, the promise of financial gain, or the pursuit of status—are losing their appeal.

Today's workforce is driven by different factors, and these changes have profound implications for how we manage and lead.

Now, the workforce—shaped by rapid technological advancements, new ways of making a living, a mind-shift toward a stronger work/life balance, and the unprecedented disruptions caused by the COVID-19 pandemic—demands a different approach.

When Tony and I discussed this, we realized that our book needed to tackle these concerns head-on. The world was already changing rapidly; and then the change was accelerated even faster by the pandemic, which not only altered the way we work but also widened the generational gap in the workplace. The new generation of workers has grown up in a technology-driven world; and their work ethic,

INTRODUCTION: NAVIGATING THE NEW WORKFORCE MINDSET

work options, and expectations are shaped by these experiences. The *Belief Windows* we and past generations have looked through have drastically changed for this new generation, which causes us all to take a new look ourselves.

I'm Michael (Mike) McDaniel, Leadership Architect™. In my thirty years as an entrepreneur and executive in corporate America, one thing has always been consistent—I am a trainer and a developer. While I have always thrived in sales, training and developing talented individuals and cultivating them to achieve their best results has always been my calling. Being connected to Tony for over twenty years has only strengthened my focus and talents. I believe value is found in the ability to solve problems, which is what has motivated me to collaborate with Tony to write this book.

Tony Jeary, The RESULTS Guy™, has impacted people's success now for over thirty years. He loves partnering with successful individuals and companies who want to supercharge their visions and make them reality even faster. His handpicked team spans generations, all working in harmony as a *High Performing Team* to study, organize his proprietary tools, and put them to work in just the right way to ensure clarity is at an all-time high.

THE EMERGENCE OF A NEW WORKFORCE

The workforce today is more diverse and technologically savvy than ever before. You may be thinking, *Well, there's a gap between Millennials and Gen X, and that was never an issue. Why should we think about it now?* The answer is simple: The gap has grown exponentially and is much bigger than ever before.

RECALIBRATE

I can remember a time when my daughter was telling me about something she wanted that was being sold online. I was very reluctant to do anything online that required a form of payment for fear that my identity would be stolen and I would have to deal with the bank and fraud departments. Once the pandemic was in full swing, the inability to get out required me to step out of my comfort zone and dive into the new era of shopping online. Now, if I don't have an Amazon package at my door at least a few times a week, I feel like I'm missing something. My daughter laughs because this is the majority of what they know and are exposed to. They don't have to adjust to the technology progression; they are growing up in an era that makes them always look to the next best thing in tech.

> **Did You Know?**
> - Baby Boomers (born 1946–1964) are typically characterized by their strong work ethic, loyalty, and preference for structured environments. They value job security and have a wealth of experience and institutional knowledge.
> - Generation X (born 1965-1980) is often seen as independent, resourceful, and adaptable, having grown up during a time of significant social and economic change. They appreciate work/life balance and are comfortable with both analog and digital technologies.
> - Millennials (born 1981–1996) are known for their tech-savviness, desire for meaningful work, and preference for

INTRODUCTION: NAVIGATING THE NEW WORKFORCE MINDSET

collaborative environments. They prioritize flexibility and continuous learning opportunities.

- Finally, Generation Z (born 1997–2012) is the first generation of true digital natives. They value diversity, innovation, and social responsibility, and they seek careers that align with their personal values.

Each generation brings unique strengths and perspectives to the table, and successful leaders must tailor their management approaches to harness these diverse contributions effectively.

Millennials and Gen Z, who now make up a significant portion of the labor market, have grown up with the internet, smartphones, and social media. Many of them graduated during the pandemic or rode out these last years in a remote learning setting. Their expectations of work/life balance, job satisfaction, and career progression differ markedly from those of previous generations. They seek meaningful work, flexibility, and opportunities for continuous learning and development.

ADAPTING VS. ADOPTING

Our goal with this book is first to provide clarity on two crucial strategies: *adapting* and *adopting*. Although we'll go into more detail on each (see chapters two and three), it's important to define them before we begin. For the purposes of this book, adapting involves modifying our existing messages and processes to better align with

RECALIBRATE

the new workforce, while adopting means embracing entirely new ways of doing things.

This concept of adapting or adopting came to me while I was at a leadership luncheon. The subject of understanding this new generation of workers came up, again. One manager of a large auto dealership spoke about how frustrated he was that he couldn't get through to his young salespeople the purpose of getting to work on time, much less fifteen to twenty minutes early. His frustration ran even further because, once the employees did show up, they wanted to grab some coffee, catch up with work peers, and then start their workday. Another business owner spoke up and said she had the same experience and has just resigned herself to understanding this is what the new workforce looks like, and she would just manage the change.

I was asked what my thoughts were. I suggested as leaders we determine what we want to adapt and what we should adopt. For example, the manager of the auto dealership knows the key to success in that business is being early to get set up, have a plan for the day, and hit the ground running. While we understand what it takes to be successful and we don't want to lower the bar (which also means we would have to lower expectations of results), we have to adapt our message as to why the younger salespeople would want to be early and how it would benefit them. The other business owner chose to adopt a different way of management because she didn't feel the change would affect results and would instead create a culture that would not only attract young workers, but would help limit attrition as well.

INTRODUCTION: NAVIGATING THE NEW WORKFORCE MINDSET

THE CHANGING LANDSCAPE

The fast pace of technological advancement, further accelerated by the pandemic, has demanded that we reevaluate our traditional work models. We must recognize as leaders that there is more involved than just having a strategy to adapt a message to get what we want. We must also understand there are new systems, technologies, and processes we should consider adopting for two critical reasons: not just to attract young, new talent but also to establish more effective and efficient ways of doing business.

The pandemic forced organizations to adopt to remote work overnight, and many discovered that it was not only feasible but also beneficial. Employees appreciated the flexibility, and employers noticed increased productivity in many cases. However, this shift also brought challenges, such as maintaining team cohesion and ensuring effective communication in a virtual environment.

The *Old Guard*, including leaders like Tony and myself, understand the foundational elements of success: *Clarity, Focus, and Execution*. However, the challenge lies in applying that methodology to bridge the gap between our tried-and-true methods and the innovative approaches embraced by the younger generation. (As a prime example, this generation prefers texting over face-to-face conversations, indicating a major shift toward more digital and less personal interactions.) It's crucial that we gain clarity about what makes this generation tick, focus on the things we can adopt or adapt to facilitate transitioning to their lifestyle and preferences while ensuring our companies thrive, and execute with the mindset of ensuring wins for everyone.

RECALIBRATE

Please note, these definitions are for the purposes of this book and may differ slightly from other accepted definitions.

Adopting: To take on or replace a new methodology, process, or technology for the purpose of effectiveness or efficiency.

Adapting: To modify or adjust an existing process, methodology, or mindset to improve outcomes while preserving the core foundation of the original concept.

HOW THIS BOOK CAN HELP

Our mission is to provide tools and insights to help leaders manage and communicate effectively with this new generation as well as recognize *Blind Spots* they may have in their organizations through management or technology. It's not just about coaching them, but also being open to learning from them. They bring valuable technological insights that can drive efficiency and innovation.

Although we suggest you read this book from cover to cover (bonus points if you have a pen in hand while you do), we also know that life can be busy. To help, we've provided a handy chapter guide, complete with the very important points (VIPs) from each. Feel free to jump to the ones that interest you most.

INTRODUCTION: NAVIGATING THE NEW WORKFORCE MINDSET

PART ONE: Why Does It Matter?

- Chapter One: The Power of Perspective

  - Effective leadership involves recognizing and addressing *Blind Spots*—areas that are often overlooked or misunderstood.
  - The principles that guide our actions are shaped by our upbringing and experiences. However, some of these principles may be outdated or incorrect. Leaders must regularly reassess and update their beliefs to ensure they remain relevant and effective in a changing world.
  - True leadership is marked by humility and the willingness to seek feedback, even from unexpected sources.
  - Understanding the perspectives of different generations and individuals is key to effective leadership. What may seem trivial to one person could be incredibly important to another.
  - Hiring top talent is important, but retaining that talent is equally crucial.

- Chapter Two: The Art of Adoption

  - Embracing new ideas and technologies is essential for staying competitive in a rapidly changing world.
  - Anticipating industry trends and adopting early can position companies as leaders.
  - Effective leadership requires abandoning outdated practices in favor of better, more effective methods.

RECALIBRATE

- A strong support system and employee feedback are crucial in selecting the right technologies and methods.
- Choose wisely between adopting new tools or adapting existing ones to maintain a strong foundation.

- Chapter Three: The Art of Adaptation

  - Key performance indicators (KPIs) are the nonnegotiable foundation for any organization's success.
  - Shifting focus from enforcing rules to fostering a positive workplace culture drives employee engagement and punctuality.
  - Effective leadership requires adapting communication and management styles to fit the diverse needs of different generations.
  - Leaders must discern when to embrace entirely new approaches versus refining existing ones to drive progress.
  - Creating a culture where feedback is actively sought and valued fosters meaningful change and inclusivity in the workplace.

- Chapter 4: Balancing Tradition and Innovation

  - In today's fast-paced world, staying still in business equates to falling behind and losing relevance.
  - Regularly assess whether your processes enhance or impede progress, and eliminate unnecessary bureaucracy.
  - Adapt your management style to meet the diverse needs and communication preferences of multiple generations.

INTRODUCTION: NAVIGATING THE NEW WORKFORCE MINDSET

- Prioritize strategic responses over emotional reactions to foster better decision-making and outcomes.
- Ensure that every new initiative or innovation aligns with and reinforces your organization's foundational principles.

PART TWO: How Do You Recalibrate?

- Chapter 5: Effective Communication
  - True collaboration involves valuing and integrating everyone's input into the outcome, especially with younger generations like Gen Z.
  - Effective communication requires choosing the right method—whether face-to-face, phone, or digital—to ensure clarity and prevent misunderstandings.
  - When managing Gen Z, it's crucial to establish from the outset that while digital communication is valuable, phone calls may sometimes be necessary.
  - Understanding employees' personal motivators through their social media and individual preferences can greatly enhance communication and collaboration.
  - Gen Z is a diverse group with varied motivators, so personalized communication is key to understanding and engaging them effectively.
- Chapter 6: The Power of Organizational Culture
  - The culture of a company is determined by how both the owner/leadership and employees perceive it, and aligning

RECALIBRATE

these perceptions is critical to attracting and retaining talent.

- Employees, particularly younger generations, rely on online platforms like Glassdoor to assess company culture, making it essential for businesses to manage their brand's online reputation.
- Strong company culture is built through transparent communication of the organization's goals and how each employee contributes to the overall success.
- Younger employees expect a stimulating and dynamic work environment, and companies must balance maintaining energy while avoiding distractions.
- Mentorship programs and regular recognition of employee contributions foster a sense of belonging and loyalty, which is crucial for long-term retention and a positive work culture.

- Chapter 7: Process-Driven Success

  - Antiquated systems not only slow down productivity but also hinder a company's ability to attract and retain top talent, especially among younger, tech-savvy employees.
  - Efficiency in processes is critical, as younger employees expect fast, streamlined workflows and become disengaged when required to navigate outdated or cumbersome systems.
  - Modern tools and technologies, such as AI and digital platforms, are essential for both improving internal

INTRODUCTION: NAVIGATING THE NEW WORKFORCE MINDSET

processes and presenting a company as forward-thinking to potential candidates.

- Clear and effective processes, combined with accountability and structure, create an environment where employees feel empowered and motivated to contribute to the team's success.
- Frustration caused by inefficient systems is the enemy of productivity, and streamlining core processes helps teams work to their full potential without unnecessary roadblocks.

- Chapter 8: Social Media as a *Force Multiplier*
  - Younger generations evaluate a company's social media presence, looking for signs of personality and engagement, which helps them determine whether the organization feels human or overly corporate.
  - Companies must maintain an active, engaging social media presence, showcasing their internal culture and using humor and relatability to appeal to younger audiences.
  - Responding transparently to both positive and negative feedback on platforms like Glassdoor is crucial, as potential employees often judge a company by how it handles criticism.
  - Social media is not only a branding tool but also a way to screen potential employees, as it gives insights into their values and lifestyle that traditional resumes may not reveal.
  - Leaders' social media presence should align with the company's values, and companies should encourage

RECALIBRATE

interaction on social platforms, creating a sense of community and engagement, both internally and externally.

PART THREE: Action Steps

- Chapter 9: Strategically Appreciating Existing Team Members

  - Creating an environment where employees want to stay, rather than sealing off the "back door," involves understanding individual motivations and providing personalized support to meet their needs.
  - A true open-door policy requires proactive leadership, where leaders reach out to employees to address concerns before they escalate, fostering trust and engagement.
  - Flexibility in addressing employee concerns, such as work/life balance, can make employees feel valued without compromising the company's standards or goals.
  - Leveraging technology and AI to track employee engagement can help anticipate potential attrition and allow for early intervention to retain top talent.
  - Closing the back door is about fostering a positive company culture where people feel valued, but also recognizing when it's time to let employees move on if they are not the right fit for the organization.

- Chapter 10: Attracting Quality Talent

  - Referrals from top employees are a powerful and often overlooked way to attract high-quality talent who are likely to align with the company's culture and values.

INTRODUCTION: NAVIGATING THE NEW WORKFORCE MINDSET

- When a top employee refers someone, they vouch for the candidate's work ethic and compatibility, increasing the likelihood of hiring the right fit and reinforcing the company's existing culture.
- Being a quality company that lives up to its promises and offers growth opportunities, respect, and alignment with employees' values is crucial for attracting top performers.
- To attract high-quality talent, companies must consistently demonstrate their positive culture and opportunities, not just claim them.
- Visibility is key in attracting talent—companies need to make it easy for potential employees to find them by maintaining a strong, proactive online presence.

PART ONE

WHY DOES IT MATTER?

CHAPTER ONE

THE POWER OF PERSPECTIVE

In the world of leadership, there's a level of humility that is essential for greatness. True leadership lies in recognizing that no matter how much experience you have or how successful you've become, there are always *Blind Spots* that can hinder your progress.

The challenges with *Blind Spots* may be that we are either so deep into a situation that we discover them too late, or we are at the top of our game, feeling invincible, and start to believe we don't have any.

Let's face it—it's so important that we uncover our *Blind Spots.* Inaccurate principles, missed distinctions, and overlooked perspectives hinder your results and your leadership capacity, no matter the generation you're dealing with.

PRINCIPLES

Let me give you an example that will bring this *Blind Spot* idea to life. Look at the picture of the FedEx truck below.

Now, we see the FedEx logo all the time, and we've seen it for years. We see it on their planes. We see it on their trucks. We see it on their packages. We see it on the internet. Yet when most people look at

RECALIBRATE

the FedEx truck, they don't see two things that are right there in front of them. Take a moment and study the logo. Can you see them? One is a serving spoon, and one is an arrow. Most people don't see them unless they've been pointed out to them before.

What this exercise reveals is that we may not even see something that has been right in front of us for a long time. That's what a *Blind Spot* is. It's something we don't see. We want to make sure we do our best to uncover our *Blind Spots* so we can make the most impactful decisions in our life.

Another layer to this is what Tony calls the *BeliefWindow*. The principles on your *BeliefWindow* filter how you see the world.

Primarily, we get the principles on our window from our upbringing—our parents. And as we go through life, the experiences, teachers, and relationships we have, as well as the information we

THE POWER OF PERSPECTIVE

get from books, the internet, and other media, keep refining those principles. All of us are doing life right now the very best we can based on our principles. Sometimes, though, a principle on our window may be wrong. In fact, I believe we're often doing life with principles that are incorrect.

Let me give you another example. Most people, maybe even you, grew up with the idea that you should always clean your plate. Right? Now, think about that. Do you think that's a good principle today? If you always clean your plate, you might struggle with portion control and you overeat. Maybe you've changed your eating habits now and you're doing well. Now let me ask you this: Do you ever feel guilty when you don't clean your plate? Many people do, because they still have that principle on their window. We know now, of course, that it's better both to use portion control and to take your plate away

RECALIBRATE

once you start getting full. Then your digestive system kicks in, and you feel satisfied. Many people get it when I use this example in talking about the *Belief Window.* Trust me on this one. You could have incorrect principles on your window. If you want the best results in your life, you must get this one right. Sometimes, we don't correct the principles on our window fast enough to keep up with technology or those around us. As technology and time move, you must update the principles on your window. **The bottom line here is that you must make sure you own the beliefs that are on your window. The truly great leaders are those who not only acknowledge their *Blind Spots* but actively seek to uncover them, even if it means asking for feedback from unexpected sources.**

DISTINCTIONS

I frequently attend leadership luncheons where we read a book and then get together to discuss the VIPs. One time, we were discussing the book *Unreasonable Hospitality* by Will Guidara. It is about a restaurant in New York that had the distinction of being ranked the number one restaurant in the world. The book, which we brought to the table for discussion, highlighted an interesting example of how the restaurant owner, despite his success, remained open to feedback and change.

The story goes that the staff at this top-ranked restaurant suggested opening on Thanksgiving Day to cater to people who might not have family to celebrate with, offering them a chance to enjoy a high-quality

THE POWER OF PERSPECTIVE

meal. Instead of dismissing the idea, the owner not only agreed but went a step further. He proposed that after the restaurant closed for the day, there would be a feast for all the employees who worked to show appreciation for their hard work.

This decision was not just about creating a positive culture—it was about the owner's willingness to listen to his team and recognize potential *Blind Spots* in his business. Despite being at the pinnacle of success, he understood that his employees, those on the front lines, could see things he might miss. This openness to feedback, even from those in the trenches, was a key factor in maintaining his restaurant's top ranking.

One of the best examples of this humility in action comes from Tony Jeary, my coauthor in this work and a leader I've worked with for over twenty years. Tony is one of the most successful and respected individuals in his field, yet he remains one of the humblest people I know. Despite his accomplishments, Tony consistently seeks out input from others, including those who might be considered less experienced or less knowledgeable.

I remember a conversation where I questioned Tony's need for feedback. "Tony, you're the guy," I said. "Why are you asking me this?" His response was simple, yet profound: "Because you're the audience, and I need to make sure that what I'm communicating is heard." Tony's willingness to seek input from someone like me, a younger colleague with a different field of expertise, demonstrated a level of humility that is rare among leaders operating at his level. He was open to being coached by anyone, from any perspective, if it made sense.

RECALIBRATE

This approach is not just a personal quirk of Tony's, it's a deliberate strategy. Tony has always been willing to put himself in a position to receive feedback, even when he's at the top of his game. He regularly sends out ideas or drafts to a group of people, asking, "What am I missing?" He actively seeks out and supports younger people, placing them in positions of authority and power within his company. He also understands the importance of staying on trend and being relevant, not just in his business strategies, but even in the little things like whether his fashion choices or the way he communicates are in line with current trends. He'll ask younger colleagues if his jeans are cool or if he's using outdated language. This might seem trivial, but it's a reflection of his commitment to staying connected with the world around him and the people he leads.

The ability to ask, "Am I still relevant?" is a powerful distinction. In the business world, particularly among the *Old Guard*, it can be difficult to maintain this kind of humility. When you've been successful for so long, there's a temptation to believe you have all the answers. But **true leadership requires a constant willingness to listen, learn from your *Blind Spots* and those around you, and adapt the principles on your *Belief Window*.**

Perspectives

When learning to lead Gen Z, it is important to remember that what might seem trivial or even absurd from your viewpoint could be incredibly important to someone else. This lesson was brought home to me during an experience I had while serving as the executive vice president of a company.

THE POWER OF PERSPECTIVE

One day, my human resources vice president came into my office with what she called "the craziest request for time off" she had ever heard. Naturally, I was intrigued. She explained that one of our employees had recently gotten a new cat and was asking for a couple of days off to help the cat acclimate emotionally to its new apartment. My first reaction was one of disbelief. I thought to myself, *This has to be the most ridiculous request I've ever encountered.*

But then, as I considered the situation further, I reflected on the employee making the request. This was someone who consistently hit his numbers, was always early, and contributed positively to our team culture. He never caused any drama and was the kind of employee any leader would value.

Faced with this unusual request, I had to decide. While it seemed foolish and crazy to me, I realized that in his world, it was neither foolish nor crazy. This was something important to him— something that mattered in his life. And when I thought about it from his perspective, it made sense to grant his request. After all, he had always done everything we asked of him, and this was a small concession to make in return.

This experience reminded me of the challenges my sixteen- year-old son faces. At my age of fifty, I often find myself minimizing the things that stress him out. What seems insignificant to me can be a source of great anxiety for him. But in his world, those things are the biggest issues he's dealing with, and they consume his thoughts and emotions. It's a powerful reminder that **perspective shapes reality.**

RECALIBRATE

Perspective shapes reality.

As leaders, we may not always understand or agree with what our employees consider necessities or legitimate concerns. But it's crucial to recognize that, from their perspective, these things are real and significant. What motivates one person might be completely different from what motivates another, and understanding this difference is key to effective leadership.

Another critical aspect of perspective in leadership is understanding the realities faced by different generations. The younger generation, particularly those entering the workforce during and after the COVID-19 pandemic, have had a very different experience compared to those who came before them. Many lost crucial years of education, personal socialization, or early career experiences, missing out on the mentorship and hands-on learning that older generations took for granted. Their reality was shaped by remote work and virtual interactions, which are vastly different from the in-office experiences of previous generations. I've noticed that younger people today are much more vocal about what they want and need from their employers. In fact, during interviews, it's no longer just the employer assessing the candidate—it's equally about the candidate evaluating whether the company aligns with their values and will provide the environment they want to thrive in. I really view it as a two-way interview these days.

THE POWER OF PERSPECTIVE

I experienced this firsthand when interviewing younger candidates. I made it a point to acknowledge that the interview was a two-way street. I told them, "I'm interviewing you to make sure you're a fit for our culture, but you're also interviewing me to ensure we provide the environment you want to be a part of." This approach resonated with my interviewees, who appreciated that I recognized their agency in the process. It's a shift in perspective that many leaders need to embrace if they want to attract and retain top talent from this generation. Remember the value to your organization of both these things: Hiring top talent is great, but retaining them is just as important.

Hiring top talent is great, but retaining them is just as important.

This generational difference also underscores the importance of listening—truly listening—to what the younger generation has to say. They are more open about their needs and expectations, and they are not afraid to speak up. As leaders, if we don't hone our listening skills, we risk missing out on valuable insights that could help our organizations thrive.

In my early career, I was fortunate to have a mentor named Norman Bircher who was an old-school salesman. Norman was gruff and could be difficult at times, but he imparted one of the most valuable lessons I've ever learned: "Hone your listening skills. You can't

RECALIBRATE

sell anybody if you don't hear what they want." This advice has stuck with me throughout my career and is just as relevant today as it was then. It's a reminder that effective leadership starts with listening— truly understanding what people need and want.

Unfortunately, the younger generation didn't get the same kind of mentorship that I did. They were thrown into the deep end during the pandemic, often without the guidance and support that previous generations received. This has created a gap in experience, but it also presents an opportunity for leaders to step up and provide the support and mentorship that these young professionals need.

Ultimately, the power of perspective lies in recognizing that every generation and every individual brings a unique viewpoint that can contribute to the success of the organization. By staying humble, open, and willing to listen, leaders can uncover hidden potential within their teams that they might have otherwise overlooked. It's about creating a culture where feedback and distinctions are valued, *Blind Spots* are acknowledged, and everyone's perspective is seen as a valuable piece of the puzzle. Remember, there is a difference between "claiming" to have a culture where feedback is valued and actually "having" that culture. An old colleague of mine, Chris Matthew, used to ask often, "How do you demonstrate that?" If you claim to have a culture where feedback is valued, you should be able to articulate how you demonstrate that. Changes made within the company based on feedback are a great way to do that.

The willingness to be coachable, even at the height of success, is what sets great leaders apart. It's easy to ignore feedback when everything seems to be going right. But the truth is, success can often

THE POWER OF PERSPECTIVE

mask underlying issues that, if left unaddressed, could lead to future problems. By maintaining an attitude of humility and openness, leaders can ensure they are not blindsided by issues they didn't see coming. It doesn't have to be lonely at the top if you follow these principles.

❚ VIPS

1. Effective leadership involves recognizing and addressing *Blind Spots*—areas that are often overlooked or misunderstood.

2. The principles that guide our actions are shaped by our upbringing and experiences. However, some of these principles may be outdated or incorrect. Leaders must regularly reassess and update their beliefs to ensure they remain relevant and effective in a changing world.

3. True leadership is marked by humility and the willingness to seek feedback, even from unexpected sources.

4. Understanding the perspectives of different generations and individuals is key to effective leadership. What may seem trivial to one person could be incredibly important to another.

5. Hiring top talent is important, but retaining that talent is equally crucial.

CHAPTER TWO

THE ART OF ADOPTION

Again, for the purposes of this book, when we talk about "adoption," we are defining it as the process of embracing new ideas, technologies, and methods that enhance effectiveness and efficiency. This definition is crucial because it emphasizes the need to continually evolve and adapt in a world that is constantly changing. During my time working with The Inline Group, I witnessed firsthand the critical role that forward thinking and the willingness to adopt new technologies and strategies played in driving success.

The Inline Group operated in an industry that was, for the most part, stuck in its ways, relying on outdated practices and reluctant to embrace change. However, what set this particular company apart was its proactive approach to innovation. They didn't just follow industry trends; they anticipated them. For instance, long before apps became ubiquitous, The Inline Group had already developed an app for its services. They were leveraging digital marketing when most of their competitors were still relying on traditional methods. This kind of foresight was instrumental in positioning them as leaders in their field.

RECALIBRATE

I recall a particular moment that encapsulated the company's forward-thinking mentality. When the idea of adopting digital marketing was first proposed, I was skeptical. I had been in the industry for a long time and didn't see the immediate need for it. However, The Inline Group didn't just want to adopt digital marketing, they wanted to own a digital marketing company. They understood the potential of digital marketing to transform their business even before the rest of the industry caught on.

Looking back, it's clear how pivotal that decision was. Digital marketing has since become the cornerstone of modern business strategies. It allows companies to target specific demographics with pinpoint accuracy, whether they're selling products, raising capital, or promoting events like comedy shows. The decision to invest in digital marketing wasn't just about keeping up with the times; it was about setting the pace.

Often, as leaders, we fall into the trap of thinking that what worked in the past will continue to work in the future. We cling to outdated methods because they're familiar and comfortable. But true leadership requires the humility to recognize when something is no longer effective and the courage to let it go in favor of something better.

I always prefer to liken it to the concept of indoor plumbing. It's hard to imagine life without it now, but at one time it was a revolutionary change that required people to abandon the old ways of doing things. Similarly, in business, we must be willing to adopt new technologies and practices that improve efficiency and effectiveness, even if it means severing ties with the past.

THE ART OF ADOPTION

This is a great way to lean into your young talent and get feedback from them and a world they are far more familiar with in many ways. It's hard to adopt new technologies if we aren't even aware they exist!

ROADBLOCKS AND RECALIBRATIONS

TOO MANY OPTIONS!

One of the biggest roadblocks organizations face when adopting new ways of doing things is simply not knowing what they don't know. Without the right support system in place, leaders can struggle to identify and implement the best options for their organization—and more importantly, for their people.

I've seen this issue play out firsthand in companies that believed they were implementing great technology, only to find that it wasn't user-friendly for their employees. Instead of integrating seamlessly, the technology created more work for the users. They had to enter the same information in different places, manually copy data from one system to another, and constantly navigate between platforms that didn't communicate with each other. What should have been a time-saving tool became a time-consuming burden. The technology might have been advanced or innovative, but it wasn't designed with the end-user in mind. As a result, the employees who were supposed to benefit from these tools ended up hating them. This is why it's crucial to have a support system in place that not only helps you identify the right technology but also ensures it's the right fit for your team.

RECALIBRATE

A good support system includes knowledgeable advisors who understand both the technical aspects of the solutions available and the specific needs of your organization. It also involves mitigating *Blind Spots* by opening the floor and actively listening to your employees—the ones who will be using the technology day in and day out. Their feedback is invaluable in determining whether a solution will truly enhance their work experience or simply add to their workload.

HIGH COST!

Adopting new technologies, systems, or processes often comes with a price tag, and as business owners, it's natural to hesitate when it comes to spending money on something that seems unnecessary. After all, if things have worked well enough without the latest innovations, why invest in them now? But the truth is, holding onto outdated methods or technologies can end up costing more in the long run. Whether it's lost productivity, inefficiencies, or missed opportunities, the hidden costs of not adopting new solutions can far outweigh the initial investment. This often means embracing the idea that you must spend money to make money. While the upfront expense might seem daunting, the long-term benefits often justify the cost. Improved efficiency, increased productivity, and better customer satisfaction are just a few of the potential returns on investment. These benefits can lead to higher profits, a stronger market position, and a more motivated workforce. The world is

THE ART OF ADOPTION

moving forward, and businesses that don't keep pace risk becoming obsolete.

ADOPT OR ADAPT?

Sometimes, just because you can adopt something doesn't always mean you should. This is where discernment and strategic thinking come into play. With so many options available, it's easy to get caught up in the excitement of the latest technology or trend. But not every new tool or system will be the right fit for your organization. Sometimes, the better approach is to adapt your existing methods rather than adopting something entirely new.

In many instances, we understand the foundations for success in our respective business. Adopting something that erodes the foundation means we have to alter expectations, which means compromising what we define as success. I've never been a part of an organization or met a business leader who wanted to lower the bar and accept below-average results.

The distinction between adoption and adaptation is vital. Adoption involves bringing in something entirely new, which can be transformative but also risky. Adaptation, on the other hand, is about refining and improving what you already have—making your existing systems and processes more effective without necessarily overhauling them. We'll dive deeper into this in the next chapter; stay tuned!

RECALIBRATE

❚ VIPS

1. Embracing new ideas and technologies is essential for staying competitive in a rapidly changing world.

2. Anticipating industry trends and adopting early can position companies as leaders.

3. Effective leadership requires abandoning outdated practices in favor of better, more effective methods.

4. A strong support system and employee feedback are crucial in selecting the right technologies and methods.

5. Choose wisely between adopting new tools or adapting existing ones to maintain a strong foundation.

CHAPTER THREE

THE ART OF ADAPTATION

As leaders, our primary responsibility is to understand the foundational principles that drive success in our organizations. These key performance indicators (KPIs) are non-negotiable; they serve as the bedrock upon which all strategies are built. However, while the foundation remains constant, the paths we take to achieve success must be flexible and responsive to the changing dynamics of our teams and environments. As I've mentioned before, this is a new era. Sometimes, the best approach is not to redefine what success looks like but rather how we journey toward it. Ask yourself: *How do I adapt either the process or the message?*

When I was at a leadership luncheon one day with the general manager of Chevrolet, he came to me, frustrated. "I know that to be successful in selling cars," he said, "you have to do X, Y, and Z. That is the foundation. It's laid, and it doesn't change. I just can't get them to *do* that."

This manager faced a common leadership challenge: knowing the foundation for success but struggling to get his team to align with it. He understood the critical actions needed to sell cars effectively—

such as punctuality, customer engagement, and proactive follow-ups—but his team wasn't meeting these expectations. They were arriving late, spending time socializing, and failing to focus on their tasks.

Initially, the manager tried to enforce these foundational standards through his traditional management style, only to end up in frustration. He then resorted to threats and shame, questioning why some employees couldn't meet the same expectations as others. However, this approach didn't yield the desired results either. This was an epiphany for me: **You cannot (and maybe even should not) always adopt a new way of success in your business.** I saw that the issue wasn't with the foundation itself; the problem was in the messaging and the culture around these expectations.

My suggestion was to do two things. First, adapt the communication style to emphasize how adopting the foundational principles of success benefits them. (This is covered in more detail in the chapter on communication.) Second, I recommended shifting the focus from imposing rules to fostering a culture where the team would naturally want to be punctual and engaged. This involved creating an environment where showing up early and being proactive were linked to a positive, enjoyable workplace culture.

I have spent a significant amount of time building a positive culture in my own workplace. My assistant feels such a strong connection to the office environment that when she's on vacation she feels like she's missing out by not being there. This sense of belonging and enthusiasm isn't driven by mandates or strict policies but by a culture that is both fun and inclusive.

THE ART OF ADAPTATION

Both Tony and I have endeavored to cultivate a workplace where employees want to show up early, not because they have to, but because they genuinely enjoy being part of the team. By fostering a light-hearted and enjoyable atmosphere, where joking and camaraderie are encouraged, we've made the office a place where people want to be, even when they have the option to be elsewhere.

Tony here! *Next Level* leaders don't just touch their employees' lives and help them improve—they truly care about them and invest their whole being into helping them be successful, whether personally or professionally. Let me give you a couple of examples:

Ella Imrie is an extremely talented young lady who worked full-time with me in The RESULTS Center while she was also going to college full time, until she moved recently to attend college in another country. (She's still working for me as my publisher remotely from there). She once told me, "Have you ever wondered why I worked for you full-time for three summers when all of my friends were out of school, having parties during the day, swimming, and just being kids? If I didn't think this was an amazing place to be, I would have quit and gone to hang out with my friends. When you can convince an eighteen-year-old to work full-time for you during the summer rather than sitting by the pool all day with her friends, you're doing something that people need to be a part of and learn from."

RECALIBRATE

> I hired Carley Crago (now Shook), the daughter of one of my friends, based solely on what I knew of her father's excellent character, as she had just finished college and had no professional experience to bring to the table. She stayed for over five years and travelled with me as my session manager. She said, "My experience with you was wonderful. It was awesome to be able to do that at such a young age, right out of college, without really having any other professional experience. I was usually the youngest person in the room, and often the only woman there as well, with quite a few presidents, CEOs, millionaires, and billionaires. It was really interesting, and it gave me the confidence to be comfortable around any type of person, no matter their status, their age, their net worth, their position, or their title."
>
> I believe it's not just about getting the job done; it's about creating a space where people feel valued and excited to be part of the team.

Work is increasingly viewed as a team effort rather than an individual pursuit. The *Old Guard* was built on individuals working in silos to stand out and advance within an organization. It was more of an individual effort to demonstrate success and ensure job security. It's now all about how the team as a whole can thrive. This requires a change in how we communicate, how we motivate, and how we integrate everyone into the broader vision of success.

THE ART OF ADAPTATION

ROADBLOCKS TO ADAPTATION AND HOW TO SOLVE THEM

YOU HAVEN'T DONE YOUR HOMEWORK

One of the significant challenges with adaptation is understanding how to effectively adapt management styles, communication methods, and even the broader organizational culture. This process is particularly difficult for those of us who are rooted in the *Old-Guard* mindset, where traditional ways of leading and interacting are deeply ingrained.

Unlike previous generations, Gen Z is more vocal about their emotions and how they feel about workplace interactions. They don't just express opinions—they share how things affect them on a personal level, which is something many leaders, particularly those accustomed to more traditional workplace dynamics, may not have encountered before. I laughed as I wrote this part because I was reminded of how much things have changed. I recalled a movie with Tom Hanks called *A League of Their Own*, where he is the coach of a woman's baseball team. In one of the scenes, Tom begins to chastise one of the players, Evelyn, for making a mistake on the field. She begins to cry after he walks away. Tom sees her cry and says, "Are you crying? There's no crying in baseball!"

To effectively manage and lead this new generation, it's essential to communicate in ways that resonate with them. This means taking the time to truly understand how Gen Z perceives and processes information, which is often more emotionally charged and transparent than what older generations might be used to.

RECALIBRATE

Leaders must acknowledge that they may not fully understand the nuances of this generational shift. Here's an example to illustrate what I'm talking about. At one point in my career, I was a partner in a digital marketing company called Valyant Digital. My partner and current owner Dan Spottsville wasn't just a digital marketing guru; he had an incredible understanding of how to connect with the younger generation. He knew exactly what they needed to thrive in the workplace.

One day, I went into the office around 9 in the morning. As I looked around, I noticed that only Dan and one other person were there. So, naturally, I asked, "Where is everyone else? When do they usually get in?" He shrugged and said, "I don't know—maybe 10:30, 11, whenever."

I was taken aback. "Whenever? What do you mean, whenever?" I was used to the traditional 8 to 5, Monday through Friday work schedule. That's when Dan said something that completely shifted my perspective.

"Mike," he said, "you have to understand this generation, especially in the creative field. They're not driven by 8 to 5 schedules; they're deadline-driven. They might wake up at midnight or 1 a.m., and that's when their creative juices are flowing. As long as they meet the deadline with quality work, does it really matter when they show up?"

It took me a moment to process that. Dan had recognized something I hadn't: the world had changed. The old 8 to 5 structure wasn't necessarily what was best anymore, especially for creatives. He saw value in letting people work when they felt most inspired, even if that meant working late at night and coming in later the next day.

THE ART OF ADAPTATION

More importantly, he understood that by giving them the freedom to work on their terms, he was getting their best work. It wasn't about being in the office at 8 a.m. anymore; it was about delivering high-quality results by the deadline. And the work we were putting out at Valyant was exceptional—head and shoulders above anything else I'd seen before.

This experience taught me that the traditional work schedule isn't always applicable in today's world. Listening to your team and understanding what works best for them can unlock their full potential. Dan recognized that, and it made all the difference in the quality of work we produced.

There are tools and resources available to help bridge gaps like these, and it's incumbent upon leaders to do the necessary homework. Understanding what motivates Gen Z, what drives their engagement, and how they interpret management decisions is crucial for making the right adaptations within the organization.

ONE-SIZE DOESN'T FIT ALL

Today, leaders face the challenge of managing multiple generations, each with distinct values, communication styles, and expectations. You're not just employing Gen Zers—you're also working with Baby Boomers, Gen Xers, and Millennials. The old approach of treating everyone the same, as if they all respond to the same incentives and communication styles, is no longer effective. It's similar to the outdated school punishment where the entire class would lose recess because of one student's bad behavior—a one-size-fits-all method that fails to recognize individual differences. In the workplace, this

RECALIBRATE

kind of blanket management approach can lead to disengagement and frustration across the board.

The solution lies in tailoring your management style to fit the specific needs and personalities of the individuals within each generation. For Baby Boomers, this might mean valuing their experience and offering more traditional communication methods. For Gen Xers, it could involve providing independence and clear expectations. For Gen Zers, it might mean fostering open dialogue and addressing their need for emotional connection and purpose at work.

By playing to the audience you're speaking to—whether it's a Baby Boomer, a Gen Xer, or a Gen Zer—you can create a more inclusive, productive, and harmonious workplace.

ADAPT OR ADOPT?

As we mentioned in chapter two, sometimes leaders adopt when they should adapt. The reverse is also true; there can be a pitfall in focusing on adapting existing practices when, in reality, we should be adopting entirely new approaches. This reluctance to let go of foundational beliefs can lead to merely tweaking or modifying outdated systems, rather than embracing the innovations that could truly drive progress. It's like putting a new exhaust system on an old Pinto—it might sound better, but it doesn't improve the overall performance.

To navigate this challenge, it's crucial to be honest with yourself and critically assess whether you're simply trying to make the old ways work or if it's time to let them go in favor of something new.

THE ART OF ADAPTATION

Sometimes, what's needed is not a mere adjustment but a complete overhaul.

A practical solution that Tony employs with great success is to actively seek feedback from a diverse group within your organization. By putting ideas out to a group of ten or fifteen people, you can gain valuable insights that may reveal the need for significant change.

Further, this concept ties back to the importance of creating a culture where feedback is not only welcomed but encouraged. When employees, especially from younger generations like Gen Z, feel that their input is valued, they are more likely to engage and contribute to meaningful change. This culture of inclusion can help address issues more effectively, ensuring that the organization evolves in ways that resonate with the entire workforce, not just a specific segment.

❚ VIPS

1. KPIs are the non-negotiable foundation for any organization's success.

2. Shifting focus from enforcing rules to fostering a positive workplace culture drives employee engagement and punctuality.

3. Effective leadership requires adapting communication and management styles to fit the diverse needs of different generations.

RECALIBRATE

4. Leaders must discern when to embrace entirely new approaches versus refining existing ones to drive progress.
5. Creating a culture where feedback is actively sought and valued fosters meaningful change and inclusivity in the workplace.

CHAPTER FOUR

BALANCING TRADITION AND INNOVATION

oday, complacency is almost impossible, and that's a good thing. With information literally at our fingertips, thanks to our phones, we're constantly connected and informed. I often joke that our phones are more social media hubs, texting tools, research devices, email connectors, and music players; and, occasionally, we may get a phone call.

Generation	Average Daily Screen Time	Proportion Who Feel Addicted
Gen Z	6 hours and 5 minutes	56%
Millennial	4 hours and 36 minutes	48%
Gen X	4 hours and 9 minutes	44%
Baby Boomer	3 hours and 31 minutes	29%

Year	Time Spent on Nonvoice Mobile Phone Use
2019	3 hours and 45 minutes
2020	4 hours and 16 minutes
2021	4 hours and 24 minutes
2022	4 hours and 30 minutes
2023	4 hours and 36 minutes

RECALIBRATE

This constant stream of information and the rapid pace of communication make it difficult to stay still; and in business, this has translated into a need for continuous movement, much like a shark that must keep swimming to stay alive. If a business becomes complacent, it's essentially signing its own death warrant.

Process cannot impede progress.

In many organizations, traditional processes are put in place with the intention of creating structure and ensuring consistency. However, as these companies strive to move forward and avoid stagnation, they often find that these very processes start to impede progress. It's a common scenario: You have to complete one report, which feeds into another report, which then leads to another layer of bureaucracy, when in reality, a simple phone call could have resolved the issue more efficiently.

The key question to ask when evaluating any process is: Does it help or hinder progress? If the steps in between are adding value and streamlining operations, then they're serving their purpose. But if these processes are becoming roadblocks that slow down decision-making and action, then it's time to reassess and change them.

BALANCING TRADITION AND INNOVATION

Complacency in Business Assessment: Red Flags

Use this assessment to identify potential areas of complacency within your business. Answer each question honestly to gauge whether your organization might be at risk of stagnation.

1. How often do you review and update your business goals?
   - (A) Regularly, at least quarterly.
   - (B) Annually or less frequently.
   - (C) Rarely, we stick to the same goals for years.
2. When was the last time you introduced a new product, service, or process improvement?
   - (A) Within the last six months.
   - (B) Within the last year.
   - (C) It's been over a year.
3. How often do you seek feedback from employees and customers?
   - (A) Regularly, and we act on it.
   - (B) Occasionally, but we don't always act on it.
   - (C) Rarely or never.
4. Do you monitor industry trends and adjust your strategies accordingly?
   - (A) Yes, we are proactive in responding to trends.
   - (B) Sometimes, but we mostly stick to what we know.
   - (C) No, we focus on what has worked in the past.
5. How adaptable is your company to new technologies?

RECALIBRATE

- (A) We eagerly adopt new technologies that improve efficiency.
- (B) We adopt new technologies slowly and cautiously.
- (C) We rarely adopt new technologies unless absolutely necessary.

6. How do you respond to competitive threats?
   - (A) We assess and respond to competitors regularly.
   - (B) We occasionally review competitors, but don't make significant changes.
   - (C) We rarely consider what our competitors are doing.

7. When was the last time you reevaluated your company's core values and mission statement?
   - (A) Within the last year, and we made updates as needed.
   - (B) Several years ago, with minor updates since then.
   - (C) They haven't been reviewed or updated in a long time.

8. Do your employees feel challenged and engaged in their roles?
   - (A) Yes, we regularly provide new challenges and development opportunities.
   - (B) Sometimes, but there are periods of stagnation.
   - (C) No, many employees seem disengaged and bored.

9. How diversified is your revenue stream?
   - (A) We have multiple revenue streams and are always exploring new ones.

BALANCING TRADITION AND INNOVATION

- ○ (B) We have a few revenue streams but rely heavily on one or two.
- ○ (C) We depend on a single revenue stream.
10. How do you handle underperforming products, services, or strategies?
    - ○ (A) We quickly assess and either improve or discontinue them.
    - ○ (B) We make slow, cautious adjustments.
    - ○ (C) We often hold on to them, hoping they'll turn around.

Scoring:

- Mostly A's: Your business is proactive and dynamic. You regularly assess and adapt, reducing the risk of complacency.
- Mostly B's: You're somewhat cautious and may be at risk of falling behind. Consider taking a more proactive approach to avoid stagnation.
- Mostly C's: Your business is likely complacent, relying too heavily on past successes. It's time to reevaluate your strategies, goals, and processes to ensure long-term viability.

The next generation, particularly Gen Z, exemplifies this anti-complacency with their demand for instant answers and quick solutions. They expect efficiency and speed in everything, from Wi-Fi connections to customer service.

RECALIBRATE

This expectation for immediacy also highlights the tension between tradition and innovation. While it's tempting to expect quick fixes and instant results, we often forget that some processes, like diagnosing a car problem, require time, careful analysis, and physical effort. We've grown so accustomed to instant information from Google or quick answers from a telemedicine consultation that we overlook the reality that some tasks simply can't be rushed.

And if you've ever tried to rush a conversation or a project when you shouldn't have, you've probably discovered firsthand just how emotions can further muddy the waters between tradition and innovation. Most of us know that it's easy to get emotionally attached, especially when you've built something from the ground up. I once worked with a company that had ambitious growth plans. After conducting an assessment, I sat down with the owner and COO to discuss the areas that needed improvement. The owner became emotional, expressing concern that she had failed her "baby," the company she had nurtured for years. I reassured her that this wasn't about failure; rather, it was about recognizing where the business could evolve to meet its growth potential.

This scenario underscores the challenge many business owners face when balancing tradition with innovation. It can be embarrassing or even disheartening to realize that certain aspects of the business are outdated. However, it's crucial to put a strategic plan in place and remove emotion from the decision-making process. This doesn't mean you should ignore emotions altogether—especially when managing a diverse workforce that includes emotional, vocal Gen Z employees—

BALANCING TRADITION AND INNOVATION

but rather, you have to know when and where to apply emotional intelligence.

Tony often talks about the concept of an *Elegant Solution* where everyone wins. To achieve this, it's essential to distinguish between strategic and emotional responses.

Emotional reactions often lead to poor outcomes, whether in business decisions or personal interactions. In contrast, taking a strategic approach allows for thoughtful consideration of what benefits everyone involved, which leads to better, more sustainable outcomes.

A strategic response is always better than an emotional reaction.

When innovating, we have to react strategically to the business situation while still being emotionally sensitive to the individual.

All that to say: Change isn't inherently good or bad, but it must be approached with a clear understanding of the pain points and foundational principles that have made the organization successful. The challenge lies in embracing new ideas and directions without alienating any generations or eroding the core values and integrity that define the company.

Tony teaches that the foundation of any organization is its bedrock—the principles, values, and strategies that have driven its success. These elements must not only remain intact but must also

RECALIBRATE

be consistently communicated and upheld. As the business landscape changes, there is a risk that, in the pursuit of innovation, the original mission can become diluted or lost. This is especially true when new initiatives or verticals are introduced without careful adherence to the guidelines and parameters initially set out.

I've seen it time and time again: Organizations attempt to diversify or expand by adding new verticals or business lines. At the outset, these new ventures are often carefully designed with clear guidelines to ensure they align with the company's mission and values. However, as implementation progresses, there is a tendency to drift from these original plans. The focus on maintaining the integrity of the new vertical can wane, leading to a misalignment between the initial vision and the final execution. The result is often disappointing performance, leaving leaders to wonder why the new venture failed to meet expectations.

In my mineral business, I've found a solution that works for me. It's simple: I adhere to a strict checklist to qualify a property before making a purchase. This checklist consists of five key criteria; and if a property doesn't meet all of them, I simply won't buy it. This approach ensures that every investment aligns with the core principles that have guided my success.

However, when I find myself compromising on these criteria— perhaps bending the rules just a bit to make a deal happen—I inevitably see a decline in the property's performance. The results don't meet my expectations, and the investment doesn't yield what it should. This situation always serves as a reminder to go back to the basics, to the original intent of my checklist, and to stick to the foundational principles that have been proven to work.

BALANCING TRADITION AND INNOVATION

Straying from these core guidelines, even in the name of flexibility or innovation, often leads to underperformance. It's a clear lesson that, while innovation is important, it must never come at the cost of the integrity and purpose that initially set the foundation for success.

I'm going to give you an example of an exercise Tony does when people come to his RESULTS studio. Tony has created a deck of cards that lists sixty different values. I've listed those sixty values for you below; and, as the exercise goes, I would like to invite you to sit down and go through them and select your top twenty values by numbering them in the spaces to the side. Now, out of those twenty, select your top ten. That doesn't mean you don't value the other things; you're just choosing the ten that mean the most to you.

Here are the sixty values:

_____ Affection _____ Alignment _____ Altruism

_____ Appearance _____ Appreciated _____ Attitude

_____ Cleanliness _____ Congruence _____ Contentment

_____ Cooperation _____ Creativity _____ Education

_____ Effectiveness _____ Efficiency _____ Fairness

_____ Faith _____ Fame _____ Family

_____ Financial Security _____ Freedom _____ Friendship

_____ Fun _____ Generosity _____ Genuineness

_____ Happiness _____ Harmony _____ Health

_____ Honesty _____ Humility _____ Inner Peace

_____ Inspiration _____ Intimacy _____ Joy

RECALIBRATE

_____ Knowledge _____ Lifestyle _____ Loved
_____ Loyalty _____ Motivation _____ Openness
_____ Organization _____ Personal Brand
_____ Personal Improvement _____ Personal Salvation
_____ Philanthropy _____ Power _____ Productivity
_____ Recognition _____ Respect _____ Results
_____ Romance _____ Routine _____ Security
_____ See the World _____ Simplicity _____ Solitude
_____ Spiritual Maturity _____ Status _____ Wealth
_____ Winning _____ Wisdom

Now, list your top ten values on a separate sheet of paper, get your phone out and take a picture of it. Save that picture. Post it. Share it with your spouse, if you're married, and with your kids. Share it with your partners. Put your values on your computer. Put them everywhere. Those are the ten primary values that you want to build your goals from and that you want to build your life from.

Now, do the same thing for your business. Of course, some values will apply better to your personal life than they will to an organization. However, this should still give you a comprehensive idea of what matters most as the foundation of your business.

So, to recap, in practice this means that every new idea or change should be measured against the company's core values and long-term

BALANCING TRADITION AND INNOVATION

goals. Leaders must ask themselves whether the proposed changes align with the organization's mission and whether they strengthen or weaken the foundation that has been laid.

❚ VIPS

1. In today's fast-paced world, staying still in business equates to falling behind and losing relevance.

2. Regularly assess whether your processes enhance or impede progress, and eliminate unnecessary bureaucracy.

3. Adapt your management style to meet the diverse needs and communication preferences of multiple generations.

4. Prioritize strategic responses over emotional reactions to foster better decision-making and outcomes.

5. Ensure that every new initiative or innovation aligns with and reinforces your organization's foundational principles.

PART TWO
HOW DO YOU RECALIBRATE?

CHAPTER FIVE

EFFECTIVE COMMUNICATION

T ony and I believe that communication must be adapted due to the diversity of the generations we now work with. From tailoring communication to how people best receive information to ensuring that the message is coming across clearly, effective communication is essential for success. It should start with the interview and remain consistent moving forward. Remember, communication is a two-way street. As owners, leaders, or managers, we must clearly communicate the organization's vision, the expectations of the position we are hiring for, and how we need this person to contribute to the company's success. We also have to listen to the feedback from employees. As we've discussed, younger generations tend to be more expressive and will speak up. When they do, listen! If a young interviewee mentions he or she dislikes rigid work hours, prefers a creative approach, and is more motivated by deadlines than a traditional eight-to-five schedule, and you hire them, can you be upset when they don't show up until nine?

While communication involves the exchange of information, collaboration goes a step further; it requires that everyone involved has

RECALIBRATE

the opportunity to present valued input and that their contributions shape the outcome. This is particularly important with the younger generations, like Gen Z, who prioritize collaborative environments where their voices are genuinely heard.

Simply talking to someone or pushing your agenda doesn't constitute collaboration; it's more akin to a dictatorship. Effective collaboration requires a balanced approach where communication is not just about transmitting information, but is more about engaging in a dialogue where all participants feel their input is respected and considered. There will, of course, be times when decisive, directive communication is necessary—when certain business decisions must be made unilaterally. However, even in these cases, it's crucial to communicate in a way that fosters a collaborative spirit, ensuring that everyone understands the reasoning and feels included in the process.

This distinction becomes even more important when considering the different methods of communication available today—texting, social media, phone calls, emails, and face-to-face interactions. Each method has its place, but there needs to be a balance. For example, while texting or emailing might be convenient, they often lack the nuance of face-to-face conversations where tone and body language play crucial roles in preventing misunderstandings.

In my personal life, I maintain boundaries to ensure meaningful communication. My sons, for instance, are not allowed to text me while we're in the same house; instead, they must come and speak to me directly. This face-to-face interaction is crucial for maintaining a strong, personal connection that isn't diluted by the impersonality of digital communication.

EFFECTIVE COMMUNICATION

In the business context, a similar approach can be beneficial. While electronic communication is necessary and efficient in many cases—such as when immediate responses are required—there's significant value in prioritizing in-person conversations. These interactions reduce the risk of misinterpretation and foster a deeper understanding between colleagues. However, it's important to clearly communicate expectations and establish boundaries for using other forms of communication when face-to-face communication isn't possible, ensuring that everyone knows how and when to use them effectively. Some Gen Zers have a noticeable aversion to picking up the phone and making calls, often preferring to communicate through texts or social media. This preference, while understandable given their comfort with digital communication, can be a challenge in a business setting where direct phone conversations are sometimes necessary.

When managing a Gen Z workforce, it's crucial to set expectations about communication methods from the very beginning. During the hiring or onboarding process, you should clearly explain that, while texting and emailing are valuable tools, there are situations where phone calls are essential, particularly when dealing with certain clientele who may prefer or expect more traditional forms of communication.

For instance, you might say something like, "I understand that in today's world, social media and texting are prevalent ways to communicate, especially for your generation. However, many of our clients are from an older generation and aren't as connected to these digital forms. To ensure we provide the best possible customer service and maintain strong relationships, we'll need to rely on phone conversations more often. This might not be your preferred method, but it's crucial for serving our clients effectively. Over time, as you build trust and relationships with them, you might be able to transition more to your preferred communication styles; but for now, we need you to meet them where they are."

The key is to communicate this expectation respectfully and explain the reasoning behind it. When you take the time to provide context and articulate the "why" behind the need for phone communication, it helps Gen Z employees understand the importance of adapting to the needs of the business and the clientele.

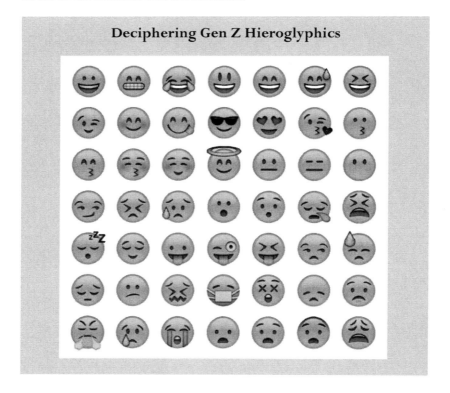

EFFECTIVE COMMUNICATION

From emojis to acronyms, texts to tweets, this generation communicates in a language that can often feel like modern hieroglyphics to those not fluent in their digital dialect. But to effectively lead and collaborate with this dynamic group, it's essential to crack the code. We've generated a fun list of some of the common abbreviations your Gen Z employees might use and what they mean. The intent of this list is NOT to make you feel old!

1. IKR—I Know, Right?
   a. Used to express agreement with something that has been said.
2. TBH—To Be Honest
   a. Used when someone is about to be frank or share their true feelings.
3. IMO/IMHO—In My Opinion/In My Humble Opinion
   a. Used to preface a personal opinion or perspective.
4. RN—Right Now
   a. Used to indicate that something is happening at this very moment.
5. IDK—I Don't Know
   a. A quick way to express uncertainty or lack of knowledge.
6. LMK—Let Me Know
   a. Used to ask someone to inform or update you about something.

RECALIBRATE

7. BRB—Be Right Back
   a. Used to indicate that someone is stepping away briefly but will return soon.
8. SUS—Suspicious or Suspect
   a. Used to describe something or someone that seems off or untrustworthy.
9. BTW—By the Way
   a. Used to introduce a new topic or add additional information.
10. JK—Just Kidding
    a. Used to indicate that a previous statement was a joke or not meant seriously.
11. DM—Direct Message
    a. Refers to a private message sent on social media platforms.
12. WYA—Where You At?
    a. Used to ask someone where they are or what they're doing.

Common Gen Z Slang

1. Lit
   a. Something that is exciting, fun, or amazing.
2. Bet
   a. Used to express agreement or confirmation, similar to "okay" or "sure."

EFFECTIVE COMMUNICATION

3. Cap
   a. A lie or something that isn't true. "No cap" means "no lie" or "for real."
4. Flex
   a. To show off or boast about something, often in a way that's meant to impress.
5. Slay
   a. To do something exceptionally well or to look amazing.
6. Woke
   a. Being aware of social issues, particularly related to justice and equality.
7. Extra
   a. Over the top, excessive, or dramatic behavior.
8. Low-key
   a. Something done subtly or under the radar; can also mean "kind of" or "sort of."

Moreover, taking the time to communicate with employees can lead to understanding them on a personal level and enhancing communication and collaboration. For example, by paying attention to their social media profiles, you can gain insights into what they care about and what motivates them. This personal connection allows you to tailor your communication in a way that resonates with them on an individual level, which can significantly improve engagement and satisfaction.

RECALIBRATE

If you want to talk about a diverse and eclectic group of people, it's Gen Z. Sometimes I'll have ten of them in the room, with ten completely different things that motivate them. So, to recap, when we talk about communication, it's important to communicate with each individual person to understand their goals and values.

Leaders can no longer just generalize and assume that everyone wants to make money. That's not true; not everyone is motivated by making a lot of money. Gen Z's motivations are different; so we need to communicate with them to understand what drives them, what their goals are, what their values are, what makes them feel like they're part of a team, and what makes them feel appreciated.

Right now, one of the biggest issues is that people don't feel appreciated. I know people who will stay in a job where they're underpaid because they feel overvalued—they feel appreciated, they feel like they contribute, and they will be as loyal as the day is long, even if you never give them a raise. I want to make it clear: this does not mean you don't need to take care of your people. What it means is that people will endure a lot for you if they feel genuinely appreciated. The only way to know that is by listening to them when they tell you what makes them feel appreciated.

The days of an entirely company-centric ideology are over. Today's workforce expects a balance between personal and professional lives, and they want to feel that their work is meaningful beyond just the company's bottom line. If a company fails to recognize this shift and continues to operate as though it's all about the company, it risks becoming a business of one—just the owner—without the support of a dedicated team.

EFFECTIVE COMMUNICATION

● VIPS

1. True collaboration involves valuing and integrating everyone's input into the outcome, especially with younger generations like Gen Z.

2. Effective communication requires choosing the right method—whether face-to-face, phone, or digital—to ensure clarity and prevent misunderstandings.

3. When managing Gen Z, it's crucial to establish from the outset that while digital communication is valuable, phone calls may sometimes be necessary.

4. Understanding employees' personal motivators through their social media and individual preferences can greatly enhance communication and collaboration.

5. Gen Z is a diverse group with varied motivators, so personalized communication is key to understanding and engaging them effectively.

CHAPTER SIX

THE POWER OF ORGANIZATIONAL CULTURE

Throughout my tenure as a leadership architect, I've visited countless companies and observed their cultures. In doing this, I've arrived at the key conclusion that when it comes to culture (among many other things), perception is reality. What this means is that if the owner perceives that the company has a good culture (or as Tony says, *Vibe*), that's their reality. If the employee perceives the culture to be poor, that's their reality. The key is to align both perspectives so that everyone is operating within the same reality. If you don't, it is going to be really challenging to attract and retain talent, regardless of their generation.

BRAND

A key aspect of this is recognizing that your company's brand carries a reputation—not just through traditional channels, but also via online platforms like Glassdoor, where employees candidly share their experiences. Many business owners underestimate how much feedback is available online about their organization and, more importantly, how younger generations are making employment decisions based on

RECALIBRATE

this feedback. In contrast to the *Old Guard*, Gen Zers are intentionally reading reviews, considering comments about culture and *Vibe*, and deciding whether your organization is a place they want to be.

I've seen a visible indicator of this shift in something as simple as the dress code. There was a time when professional attire meant a tie, button-up shirt, and slacks. Today, expectations are more relaxed; and you might find employees (and even C-Level executives like Tony and me!) wearing jeans, leather shoes, and a sports coat—yet still being considered appropriately dressed. When I attended conferences to speak, I would also help man the booth in the exhibit hall. On one occasion, I decided not to wear my suit and instead opted for a nice pair of jeans, leather shoes, and a sport coat. To my surprise, we had significantly more traffic than usual. I began asking people what attracted them to the booth, and their responses were consistent: I didn't look like a salesman waiting for the next pitch. It turned out the suit actually worked against me! As mentioned earlier in the book, relevancy is crucial to showing employees that your organization is in touch with modern trends and open to evolving norms, rather than being stuck in old-school thinking. Allowing some flexibility in the dress code, for instance, gives employees the freedom to express themselves within professional boundaries. While it's clear they can't show up in SpongeBob pajamas, offering room for personal style—within what is professionally acceptable—helps create a culture where people feel comfortable and valued while still maintaining a sense of professionalism. This balance not only supports individual expression but also reinforces a more progressive, adaptive work environment.

THE POWER OF ORGANIZATIONAL CULTURE

COMMUNICATION

When we talked about leadership, we emphasized that a key factor in building a strong culture is clear communication of the company's goals, mission, vision, and strategic objectives. It's about ensuring that employees understand how they fit into the bigger picture and feel like an essential part of the success formula. This approach ingrains them into the culture, showing that they're not just valuable as individuals but crucial to the overall success of the team. Younger generations, in particular, value this sense of community. When they can see how their contributions help move the entire organization forward, it creates a stronger sense of belonging, much like the microcommunities we see on platforms like Facebook. Within Facebook, for example, you find smaller, vibrant communities—whether around Jeeps, fitness, or other shared interests. Similarly, people in the workplace, especially younger employees, are seeking that sense of being part of something larger.

In the past, communication was more directive: "This is where the company is headed, and this is your job." Employees were expected to understand their role and go along with it. Today, however, it's about fostering collaboration and showing the team what we are collectively trying to achieve. This shift in communication—explaining how each person fits into the team's overall success—helps create a culture where employees feel ingratiated into the company's mission. In some organizations, leaders believe they have a great culture; but when you look at the faces of the people on the sales floor, their expressions tell a different story—one of disengagement. To build a truly great culture, employees need to feel involved, valued, and integral to the company's broader vision.

RECALIBRATE

One effective way to gauge and improve this is through feedback. Anonymous surveys, like those offered by platforms such as SurveyMonkey, can provide valuable insights into how employees truly feel about the culture. But gathering feedback is just the first step. Leaders must be willing to act on that feedback and make necessary changes, even if the results aren't what they expected. A creative way to track this cultural progress is through word clouds. During meetings, employees can anonymously submit one word that they feel describes the current culture. Over time, leaders can compare these word clouds to see how the culture is evolving and whether improvements are being made. It's a simple, yet effective, method to keep a pulse on how employees are feeling and to demonstrate transparency and commitment to positive change.

FAST PACED

For the younger generation, who are accustomed to fast-paced, highly stimulating environments, the workplace must match that level of energy. They are used to multitasking—watching TV, playing video games, and listening to music all at once. When something is missing from that stimulation, they notice immediately. In the same way, they seek that constant engagement in their work environments. The challenge for organizations is to create a fast-paced culture that energizes employees without causing distractions. It's about keeping the environment stimulating and dynamic, yet focused enough to achieve goals effectively.

THE POWER OF ORGANIZATIONAL CULTURE

HOW DO YOU RECALIBRATE?

One powerful strategy to adjust your company's culture is to form a *Culture Committee*. This committee, comprised of nonmanagement employees from different departments, represents the voice of the workforce. They can provide feedback on what activities or initiatives would truly engage the team. Too often, management plans events that they believe employees will enjoy, only to find out that there's little interest. By letting the employees themselves have a say, the organization can plan activities that resonate more deeply and foster a stronger sense of community.

Mentoring is another cornerstone of a healthy workplace culture. It's the difference between throwing someone into the water and telling them to swim and jumping in the water with them to show how it's done. Mentorship programs foster a sense of belonging, showing employees that the organization is invested in their growth and success. It's about walking alongside employees, guiding them, and helping them thrive within the company. This builds trust and loyalty, which are essential components of a positive culture.

Recognition is equally vital. Younger generations, in particular, want to feel appreciated for their efforts. While financial compensation is important, recognition goes beyond a paycheck. Whether it's through formal awards, public acknowledgment, or peer-to-peer nominations, recognizing individual contributions helps to reinforce the value that employees bring to the team. Encouraging employees to nominate their peers for recognition also creates a culture of mutual respect and appreciation, further strengthening the community within the organization.

TYING IT ALL TOGETHER

If employees don't feel a sense of belonging, they often disengage and check out. Interestingly, I've noticed this trend starting to affect not just younger workers but even older employees, who may see the recognition and sense of community enjoyed by younger generations and begin to feel like they're missing out on something special. Gone are the days when employees, like my great-grandfather, worked for a company like Campbell Soup for forty-one years. In today's workforce, tenure of five or six years is considered quite good.

The key to longer retention is creating that great culture. Even if an employee might have originally planned to leave after a year, you could possibly extend their tenure to five or even ten years by making them feel like they are part of something meaningful. This sense of belonging not only increases job satisfaction, but also minimizes turnover. As we discussed earlier, platforms like Glassdoor can reveal whether your company has a high turnover rate, which can be a major red flag to potential hires. If people see that your company has a revolving door of employees, it raises concerns and sets the expectation that the job is merely a temporary bridge to something better.

As leaders and business owners, we need to focus not only on attracting the best talent but also on keeping them. It doesn't matter how many great employees come in through the front door if we don't close the back door. Building a strong culture and making employees feel valued is crucial to ensuring that they stay and contribute to the long-term success of the company.

THE POWER OF ORGANIZATIONAL CULTURE

 VIPS

1. The culture of a company is determined by how both the owner and employees perceive it, and aligning these perceptions is critical to attracting and retaining talent.

2. Employees, particularly younger generations, rely on online platforms like Glassdoor to assess company culture, making it essential for businesses to manage their brand's online reputation.

3. Strong company culture is built through transparent communication of the organization's goals and how each employee contributes to the overall success.

4. Younger employees expect a stimulating and dynamic work environment, and companies must balance maintaining energy while avoiding distractions.

5. Mentorship programs and regular recognition of employee contributions foster a sense of belonging and loyalty, which is crucial for long-term retention and a positive work culture.

CHAPTER SEVEN

PROCESS-DRIVEN SUCCESS

Theorists say that we're currently entering the age of Industry 4.0, something which, in short, is akin to the Fourth Industrial Revolution. Industry 4.0 is categorised by tension between sticking to antiquated systems and embracing modern technology. In my work with businesses that rely on outdated systems, I frequently hear the same feedback, especially from younger employees: They know there are better ways to get things done. Often, they've worked at companies with more efficient systems but left because of poor culture. When you have an outdated system, it not only impacts efficiency, but also your ability to attract top talent. And if you look at Glassdoor reviews, younger employees are quick to point out that a company is "old school" or "stuck in the past." That's not the kind of reputation that will draw the best candidates, and it certainly won't retain the top talent you already have.

THE COST OF ANTIQUATED SYSTEMS

Relying on outdated systems is like using a horse and buggy in the age of electric cars. Sure, it will get you where you need to go, but not

RECALIBRATE

without a lot of extra effort, time, and frustration. You can't demand modern results from an outdated system, nor can you expect your team to deliver at the same level as your competitors if you aren't providing them with the right tools. It's asking someone to work three times harder to achieve the same results that someone else accomplishes with far less effort, thanks to modern technology.

A recent trip to Seattle really brought this idea home for me. We found that taxis were cheaper than Uber, but then we came across a guy with a motorized bicycle cart. He was actually more expensive than the taxi or the Uber, but we thought we would give it a try. We discovered he could take shortcuts through parking lots and sidewalks, bypassing the usual traffic routes. Not only did he get us to our destination faster than a taxi could have, but the ride was also more enjoyable. He shared insights about the city and suggested places to visit, and we even had a more personal experience along the way. This made me realize that there are more efficient ways of doing things, often better than you initially imagine, and they can even add unexpected value along the way. Efficiency isn't just about getting there faster; it can also enhance the experience itself. The added expense was worth the cost!

When it comes to streamlining core processes, this same principle applies, especially with the younger generation. They expect immediate results and efficient systems. The days of using the Dewey Decimal System are long gone; today, younger workers will just Google something in a matter of seconds. That's how they're wired, and that's the kind of efficiency they expect in the workplace. If your core processes are slow, cumbersome, or require unnecessary steps,

PROCESS-DRIVEN SUCCESS

you're going to lose their engagement. They want efficiency, and they want answers fast. If they're spending time navigating multiple systems that don't communicate with each other, they'll quickly become frustrated, which will eventually impact their productivity and your company culture.

I've seen this firsthand in my own experience. I subscribe to services that summarize entire books in minutes. I get the key takeaways and essential information without spending hours reading the full book. If I like what I see, I can always buy the full book and dive deeper. This is how the younger generation operates; they value efficiency and prioritize quick access to information. If your internal processes aren't streamlined, you risk frustrating them and losing their buy-in.

In the digital marketing world, for instance, many workers don't operate on a strict nine-to-five schedule. They're driven by deadlines. If they can finish a project in an hour, they see no reason to stay at their desk for the rest of the day. They want the freedom to complete their tasks efficiently and then use their time as they see fit.

This brings me to a key point: meetings about meetings. How many times have you sat in a meeting, waiting for your turn, only to realize that the majority of the discussion didn't apply to you? You sit there, knowing that only a few minutes of the entire meeting pertain to your responsibilities; yet your time is tied up for an hour or more. This is a great example of how core processes can be streamlined. Instead of holding seven people in a meeting where only eight minutes of it is relevant to one person, why not rethink the approach? If you, as a leader or manager, need specific updates or have questions for

RECALIBRATE

one individual, you can simply reach out to that person directly for clarity, feedback, or coaching. This way, you're not wasting everyone's time in a broad meeting but still ensuring that all important points are addressed efficiently. The same goes for core processes. If your systems are convoluted, whether in sales, customer service, or operations, you'll lose the younger generation's engagement. They're looking for streamlined workflows that help them work smarter, not harder.

Here's an example to help you really understand this. I once worked at a company where I had to pull information from one database, then move to another database for the rest of the data, and finally combine everything manually in a third system to get the full picture. The databases didn't speak to each other, turning what should have been a simple task into a frustratingly time-consuming process. At fifty years old, I was frustrated by the inefficiency; so you can imagine how a twenty-something-year-old raised in a digital-first world would feel. They would be even more frustrated and less willing to stay engaged if they had to deal with that on a daily basis.

To avoid this, leaders need to ask themselves: Are we doing this in the most efficient way? Are we using the best tools available? If the answer is no, it's time to reconcile your internal processes and make the necessary updates. Streamlining isn't just about making life easier for your team; it's about retaining their engagement, ensuring productivity, and fostering a workplace culture that values efficiency. Ultimately, if you want more out of your people, you have to provide them with the tools and systems that allow them to deliver at their best.

PROCESS-DRIVEN SUCCESS

ATTRACTING THE RIGHT TALENT WITH MODERN TOOLS

To attract younger generations who are often more technologically savvy, companies must offer the tools and systems that meet their expectations. Tools like Excel, Calendly, Prezi, Canva, and even AI are not just "nice to have"; they are essential for drawing in the best candidates. Modernizing your systems isn't just about giving employees tools to perform better; it's about presenting your company as forward-thinking. And it's not just the technology itself; how you use it matters too. Artificial intelligence (AI), for instance, can help you not only with internal processes, but also with recruiting, marketing your job opportunities, and finding the right candidates.

However, it's important to remember that the process cannot impede progress; and this is critical when we think about how we change the way we do business or communicate. The distinction between adapting and adopting is crucial here. The core message of this book is that, while it's important to adopt new tools and processes or adapt old ones, the ultimate measure of success is whether or not these changes are delivering results. If we're constantly adapting without data to back up our progress, we have to step back and reassess. At the end of the day, the data will tell us if we're on pace, falling behind, or moving in the right direction. It's essential to let the results speak for themselves rather than changing things for the sake of change.

I've walked into many organizations where the leadership wanted to move the company in a different direction because revenue wasn't where they wanted it to be. What I often found was that things were

RECALIBRATE

too lax: Processes needed tightening, and accountability had fallen by the wayside. It reminded me of being in school. At the start of the year, you had the cool teacher who let you get away with a lot. But as more students started to fail, they had to crack down; and by the end of the year, everyone hated that teacher. Then, there was the strict teacher who set clear guidelines from day one. Over time, as students understood the boundaries and expectations, this teacher was able to step back and relax the rules; and in the end, everyone appreciated the structure and guidance.

There's a lesson here for business leaders: Structure, processes, and accountability are important; but they have to be balanced with a culture that people enjoy being a part of. Community, culture, and teamwork thrive when there are clear guidelines and expectations, but also when people feel a sense of belonging and purpose. Employees need to understand the rules they're working within but also feel like they're contributing to a larger goal. It's that balance between structure and culture that leads to success.

The key is to set up the right processes, give your team the tools they need to succeed, and ensure they understand the expectations. But just like that teacher who could ease up once the students knew the rules, leaders must find that balance between enforcing guidelines and fostering an environment where people want to work and contribute to the team's success.

At the end of the day, frustration is the enemy of productivity; and if your systems are frustrating, you'll struggle to get the best out of your people. By streamlining your core processes, you can ensure that

PROCESS-DRIVEN SUCCESS

your team is working at their full potential, delivering results quickly and efficiently without unnecessary roadblocks.

❚ VIPS

1. Antiquated systems not only slow down productivity, but also hinder a company's ability to attract and retain top talent, especially among younger, tech-savvy employees.

2. Efficiency in processes is critical, as younger employees expect fast, streamlined workflows and become disengaged when required to navigate outdated or cumbersome systems.

3. Modern tools and technologies, such as AI and digital platforms, are essential for both improving internal processes and presenting a company as forward-thinking to potential candidates.

4. Clear and effective processes, combined with accountability and structure, create an environment where employees feel empowered and motivated to contribute to the team's success.

5. Frustration caused by inefficient systems is the enemy of productivity, and streamlining core processes helps teams work to their full potential without unnecessary roadblocks.

CHAPTER EIGHT

SOCIAL MEDIA AS A FORCE MULTIPLIER

When it comes to attracting younger generations, social media plays a pivotal role. Today, potential employees check to see if a company has a presence on platforms like Facebook, Instagram, and Twitter. They want to see what kind of message the company is putting out and how it engages with the world. Does the company have personality? Does it feel human, or is it cold and corporate?

I always laugh when I think about how Wendy's became famous on social media. Whoever was running their marketing during that period nailed it—self-deprecating humor, clever jabs at the competition, and a playful tone that showed they weren't afraid to be bold and a little cheeky. This kind of social media presence shows a company's progressiveness and forward-thinking nature, something that greatly appeals to younger generations. It's a lesson for all businesses: If you want to attract the best young talent, you need to adapt your message and show personality on social media.

Your social media pages can't be dry or sterile; they need life and character. Put someone in charge who knows how to speak the language of your target audience. Showcase your company functions,

RECALIBRATE

highlight employee successes, and make the page an extension of your company's vibrant culture. Encourage employees to interact with these pages and get involved in the social media conversation. When a company's social media reflects a strong, engaged community, it helps build that same community, internally and externally.

When we think about platforms like Glassdoor, it's easy to lump them in with social media; but in reality, they are much more than that. Glassdoor is a digital tool that allows companies to receive valuable feedback from current and former employees and, most importantly, demonstrate how they respond to that feedback. The responses to Glassdoor reviews can be even more critical than the reviews themselves because they reveal how the company handles both praise and criticism.

During my time at a company with numerous Glassdoor reviews, I made it a point to approve all responses. Whether it was a positive review such as, "This company has a great culture and is very progressive," or a negative one, we responded to each. For positive reviews, we made sure our human resources team emphasized that our success came from listening to feedback and being adaptable, constantly learning from our team's contributions. For negative reviews—where disgruntled employees might complain about unfair expectations—our responses were equally deliberate. You can't control what people say, and you certainly can't respond with anger. Instead, it's essential to highlight that the company's culture and community set high standards; and while it may not be the right fit for everyone, that's what makes the company successful.

SOCIAL MEDIA AS A FORCE MULTIPLIER

This type of transparent engagement shows potential employees, especially younger generations, that you're responsive and committed to maintaining a healthy work culture. Negative feedback is inevitable, but what matters most is how you handle it. When a company shows that it's open to feedback and willing to address issues, it sends a message that leadership cares about the work environment. For the younger workforce, this is crucial. They don't just read the complaint; they focus on how the company responds, which tells them more about the company's values than the complaint itself.

SOCIAL MEDIA AS A TOOL FOR SCREENING

But social media isn't just about projecting your brand; it's also a powerful tool for screening candidates. Whenever I was considering hiring someone, I'd check their Facebook, Instagram, and Twitter pages. This gave me a clearer picture of who they truly were. If a person's social media was filled with pictures of them constantly partying or engaging in questionable behavior, I could get a sense of whether they'd be a good cultural fit for the company.

That's not to say we should judge people solely based on their social media presence, but it provides insights that a resume or personality test can't. Many people, especially younger generations, curate their social media profiles intentionally. It's not just random—it's how they want to present themselves to the world. If someone's page is filled with wild parties, it tells you something about their priorities. On the other hand, some people carefully craft a "perfect" online persona; and

RECALIBRATE

while that's fine, it's worth recognizing that it might not be the full picture of who they are.

We also need to ensure that our leadership's social media presence aligns with the company's values. If the CEO's personal page is filled with polarizing content, it can undermine all the work the company is doing to present itself positively online. Leaders are an extension of the brand, and their personal pages need to reflect that.

BUILDING AN INTERACTIVE SOCIAL MEDIA CULTURE

One of the keys to successful social media is making sure it's interactive. There's nothing worse than seeing a company with a polished Instagram page that has very few followers or engagement. It creates a disconnect. To avoid this, encourage your employees to interact with the company's social media posts. When employees engage, whether by commenting or sharing content, it reflects the camaraderie and community within the company. A company's social media presence isn't just about the brand, it's about showing the world the team behind it and demonstrating the internal culture.

Social media also provides opportunities for leaders to engage with their employees on a more personal level. For example, if one of your employees posts about a vacation or an exciting experience, jump into the comments and ask about it. This simple interaction shows you care about their life outside of work and builds a stronger connection. It also allows you to leverage social media to create a deeper company culture that extends beyond the office.

It's also important to recognize that younger generations, particularly Gen Z, often know how to utilize social media better than

SOCIAL MEDIA AS A FORCE MULTIPLIER

older generations. There's no shame in asking for help or feedback from your younger employees when rolling out a new Instagram aesthetic or launching a social media campaign. They are often more in tune with the trends and expectations of online audiences. If you're unsure whether your message will resonate, ask your team for input. They'll likely know what works and what doesn't—and they'll also know what's no longer acceptable or might come across as outdated.

● VIPS

1. Younger generations evaluate a company's social media presence, looking for signs of personality and engagement, which helps them determine whether the organization feels human or overly corporate.

2. Companies must maintain an active, engaging social media presence, showcasing their internal culture and using humor and relatability to appeal to younger audiences.

3. Responding transparently to both positive and negative feedback on platforms like Glassdoor is crucial, as potential employees often judge a company by how it handles criticism.

4. Social media is not only a branding tool, but also a way to screen potential employees, gaining insights into their values and lifestyle that traditional resumes may not reveal.

RECALIBRATE

5. Leaders' social media presence should align with the company's values; and companies should encourage interaction on social platforms to create a sense of community and engagement, both internally and externally.

PART THREE

ACTION STEPS

CHAPTER NINE

CLOSING THE BACK DOOR

When we talk about "closing the back door" in a company, it doesn't mean sealing it shut so that no one ever leaves. Rather, it's about creating an environment where employees want to stay while recognizing that some people may naturally move on. Some employees you bring in through the front door may turn out to be incredible people with great talent; but as you work with them, you might realize that their best talents are not aligned with your organization's needs. This is why the back door must have a hinge—it should open and close when it's best for both the company and the employee.

INTENTIONALITY IN RETENTION

The first step in closing the back door is being intentional about creating a company that is worth staying in. To understand this, you need to talk to your people. Your team is your best source of information on what's working, what's not, and what could be improved. Creating an environment where employees feel valued, heard, and appreciated is essential. One of the most effective ways to ensure you're closing that back door is by building a workplace

RECALIBRATE

culture that makes employees want to stay. There is an easy way to grade ourselves as leaders on how well we do this, but the reality of the answer is not always pleasant. Is your company a revolving door of new employees or is there a lasting tenure among them?

But there's even more to it than that. Recognizing the people you want to stay is key to this strategy. Invest intentionally in those individuals, both in terms of professional growth and personal support. For instance, if you know that someone is a person you want to keep in the company, you have to make a conscious effort to understand what drives them and what they value. This goes beyond general perks or team-wide initiatives; it's about understanding and supporting individuals on a personal level. Whether it's with career advancement, work/life balance, or personal growth, tailoring your efforts to each employee's motivations will make a significant difference.

One effective way to reduce attrition is by ensuring you have a true open-door policy. Company leaders often claim to have open doors, where employees are welcome to come and share their thoughts, concerns, or ideas. But how often do people actually feel comfortable walking into their boss's office to discuss real issues? Many don't. In fact, that open door often becomes symbolic, with employees hesitating to use it for fear of repercussions or being misunderstood.

This is where proactive leadership comes in. Rather than waiting for employees to bring issues to you, sometimes you need to go to them. Just like in customer service, where reaching out to address issues before they escalate can diffuse difficult situations, approaching employees to discuss potential challenges can prevent small

CLOSING THE BACK DOOR

frustrations from festering. Employees appreciate it when leaders take the initiative to check in with them, showing that they are valued and their concerns are heard.

When you do this, don't approach it with a mindset of dismissal. If someone expresses frustration to you, the instinct might be to think, *They are the problem*, and move to let them go. But instead, ask whether there's something deeper going on. Is it really that individual, or could there be a larger issue within the company that needs addressing? If one employee feels this way, chances are others do too. By engaging with employees early and often, you can avoid letting issues grow and instead find solutions that work for both the employee and the organization.

While you want to be flexible in addressing employee concerns, there's a balance to be struck. Adapting to individual needs doesn't mean lowering the organization's standards or compromising the company's integrity. It's important to hold on to the goals and values that make the company successful. However, within those boundaries, there's usually room for compromise or adjustment that can make an employee feel valued and engaged without sacrificing the team's broader goals.

For example, if someone has concerns about their work/life balance or feels they need more flexibility, work with them to find a solution. Flexibility and personalization in problem solving can go a long way toward making employees feel they're in the right place. The idea is to keep the back door closed by creating a space where employees feel their needs are being met, while maintaining the high standards that drive the company forward.

RECALIBRATE

USING TECHNOLOGY TO STAY AHEAD OF ATTRITION

Leveraging technology, including AI, is another way to anticipate and address attrition. There are tools available that can analyze employee engagement and predict when someone might be at risk of leaving, based on their behaviors and responses to surveys or feedback. AI can help spot patterns and trends that might not be immediately obvious to managers, allowing leaders to intervene before an employee reaches the point of no return.

An open-door policy can be supplemented with proactive data analysis, allowing you to make better decisions and retain valuable employees. For example, if AI detects that someone's productivity or engagement is declining, it could prompt a manager to have a conversation with that person before they consider leaving.

In the end, closing the back door is about more than just preventing attrition; it's about creating an environment where people want to stay—a community—but also recognizing when it's time to open that door and let people move on. Not everyone will fit perfectly within the team, and that's okay. What's important is that you're intentional in creating a company culture where people feel valued and want to contribute, and that you're proactive in addressing concerns before they lead to turnover.

CLOSING THE BACK DOOR

 VIPS

1. Creating an environment where employees want to stay, rather than sealing off the "back door," involves understanding individual motivations and providing personalized support to meet their needs.
2. A true open-door policy requires proactive leadership, where leaders reach out to employees to address concerns before they escalate, thereby fostering trust and engagement.
3. Flexibility in addressing employee concerns, such as work/life balance, can make employees feel valued without compromising the company's standards or goals.
4. Leveraging technology and AI to track employee engagement can help anticipate potential attrition and allow for early intervention to retain top talent.
5. Closing the back door is about fostering a positive company culture where people feel valued, but also recognizing when it's time to let employees move on if they are not the right fit for the organization.

CHAPTER TEN

ATTRACTING QUALITY TALENT

Attracting top talent requires more than just a strong social media presence or a reputation for innovation (which we've talked about in previous chapters). While these aspects are important, referrals and being a quality company are equally critical, if not more so. Referrals are often an overlooked strategy for bringing in high-quality candidates, but they can be one of the most effective ways to strengthen your workforce. Additionally, being a company that truly lives up to its promises and creates a workplace where people want to be is the foundation for long-term success.

THE POWER OF REFERRALS

One of the most powerful ways to attract quality talent is through referrals from your top employees. If you have someone who is a rockstar within your company—consistently demonstrating dedication, talent, and a strong cultural fit—chances are they surround themselves with like-minded people. People tend to associate with those who share their values, work ethic, and sense of responsibility. An employee like that is not likely to be spending their time with individuals who regularly no-show, skip around, or demonstrate a lack of commitment. Their community is probably filled with other high performers.

Tapping into this network can be a game changer. Referral-based hiring brings in candidates who are more likely to align with your company's values and culture, because they come from a trusted source. When a top employee refers someone, they are essentially vouching for that person's work ethic and compatibility with the company. This not only increases the likelihood of hiring the right person, but also strengthens the sense of community within your existing team.

By hiring from within the community of your top employees, you're not just adding new talent; you're reinforcing the culture you've already worked hard to create. The new hires are more likely to integrate smoothly, share the same work ethic, and contribute to the positive environment that attracted them in the first place.

BEING A QUALITY COMPANY

Another crucial factor in attracting quality talent is to simply be a quality company. Top talent is drawn to workplaces where they see opportunities for growth, respect, and alignment with their personal values. It's not enough to claim you're a great place to work—you have to demonstrate it consistently.

Top performers don't want to waste time on companies that don't live up to their promises. They want to work for organizations that back up their claims of culture, innovation, and support with tangible action. If you want to attract and retain the best, you need to be the kind of company they're eager to join.

ATTRACTING QUALITY TALENT

The goal should be for them to seek you out. When you become the type of company that high performers talk about positively, you'll attract top talent without having to search as hard. That said, being a quality company isn't a static achievement—it requires constant intentionality. You have to continuously invest in your people, refine your processes, and maintain a culture that people want to be part of.

MAKE IT EASY TO BE FOUND

A crucial point in attracting talent is making it easy for them to find you. Even if you're the best company to work for, if no one knows who you are, you won't be attracting top talent. The visibility of your company plays a major role in this process, especially in a world where online presence is key.

PLAY NICE IN THE SANDBOX

Make it a point to build great relationships with your competitors. In my experience, having strong relationships with competitors has always been more beneficial than a deterrent. I could call them to exchange insights that helped us both. And if a top producer or employee wanted to leave, where do you think they preferred to go? A great culture doesn't have to exist only within the walls of your organization.

Attracting quality talent isn't about waiting for the right people to knock on your door—it's about being proactive, intentional, and visible. When you put the right systems in place, the top talent will come looking for you.

RECALIBRATE

 VIPS

1. Referrals from top employees are a powerful and often overlooked way to attract high-quality talent who are likely to align with the company's culture and values.

2. When a top employee refers someone, they vouch for the candidate's work ethic and compatibility, increasing the likelihood of hiring the right fit and reinforcing the company's existing culture.

3. Being a quality company that lives up to its promises and offers growth opportunities, respect, and alignment with employees' values is crucial for attracting top performers.

4. To attract high-quality talent, companies must consistently demonstrate their positive culture and opportunities, not just claim them.

5. Visibility is key in attracting talent—companies need to make it easy for potential employees to find them by maintaining a strong, proactive online presence.

CONCLUSION

The most important thing I want to emphasize is how crucial it is for us, as leaders and business owners, to remain open to change. Whether it's adapting to new trends or adopting new technologies, the world is constantly shifting—be it generational changes or technological advances. As leaders, we must have the humility to recognize that we have *Blind Spots*. No matter how experienced or knowledgeable we are, we won't always have all the answers. The truth is that with the rise of AI, our inability to "have all the answers" increases. We might rely more on machines than we ever thought possible.

However, in the process of building our businesses—whether it's shaping our social media presence, crafting company culture, or defining personal and corporate brands—it's critical not to lose sight of the human element. At the end of the day, it's recognizing the value of people that makes businesses thrive. In a world moving at breakneck speed, with technology advancing faster than we can keep up, it's easy to lose touch emotionally. But maintaining that emotional connection with our teams, customers, and communities is what will truly set companies apart.

RECALIBRATE

As much as we might rely on technology in the future, people are at the heart of every business. It's not enough to have the latest tools or the most efficient systems if we lose our ability to connect, to empathize, and to recognize the humanity in each other. The key to navigating the future successfully will not just be adopting AI or leveraging the latest trends; it will be staying real in how we communicate, lead, and engage with others.

Keeping that authentic connection alive, both with ourselves and our people, is the path to long-term success. Technology will continue to evolve, but the businesses that remain grounded in authenticity, empathy, and human connection will be the ones that truly flourish in the changing world.

ABOUT THE AUTHORS

TONY JEARY

Tony has impacted people's success now for over thirty years. Like a top professional athlete preparing for competition, Tony takes each assignment, engagement, and/or partnership with extreme seriousness. Tony likes to win, and he wins by helping others win. He chooses carefully the people and organizations he works with and then goes all in, focusing on what will provide the highest/*Next-Level* return on effort. He and his handpicked team research, study, and organize his proprietary tools to put them to work in just the right way to ensure clarity is at an all-time high. The next step zeros in on identifying and focusing on the key *Force Multipliers*, followed, of course, by inspiring measurable execution.

Tony is a prolific author, with most of his titles (over one hundred books!) focused on helping others get *RESULTS Faster*! He and his team work mainly in his unique, private RESULTS Center, located just a few

RECALIBRATE

minutes north of Dallas-Ft. Worth Airport, which houses his thirty-plus years of *Best Practices*, courses, and tools.

He is blessed with an awesome family, whom he loves on, prays for, and nourishes daily. His friendships are many; he thrives on making their lives better. He's an encourager to the world and is committed to an ever-growing Rolodex that numbers in the tens of thousands.

He loves partnering with the successful who want to supercharge their visions and make them reality even faster.

His life has amazing favor from God, and he's prayerfully thankful. He's all about *Next-Level* everything. As a keynoter, he enjoys wowing audiences and making events memorable. His sweet spot is strategic planning, and he invests most of his professional time helping his partners thrive.

He can be reached at info@tonyjeary.com or 817.430.9422.

MIKE MCDANIEL

Mike has spent his entire career in sales and training. Early in his life, he recognized his gift for developing people to reach their full potential. Over the years, he has trained hundreds of successful salespeople, managers, and business owners. Mike has spoken in front of thousands of people, encouraging them to gain clarity and achieve success. His commitment to personal growth has fostered a relationship with his business coaches, Joe Kesterson and Tony, for over 20 years. Mike is

ABOUT THE AUTHORS

also the owner of Matrix Epoxy and Woodlands Capital Solutions.

He feels blessed to have a family that supports and encourages him to follow his own path and continually refine who he is. Mike is surrounded by friends, who he considers extended family, with relationships spanning over 40 years. He brings boundless energy and positivity to everyone he encounters.

His faith, family, and friends are the reasons he gives thanks every day for a blessed life.

WHAT WE CAN DO FOR YOU

TJI

Results Coaching

Advice Matters, if it's the right advice. Having coached the world's top CEOs, published over 100 books, and advised over 1,000 clients, Tony has positioned himself with a unique track record to take serious high achievers to a whole new level of results.

Interactive Keynotes

Tony not only energizes, entertains, and educates, but he also has his team work strategically and smartly with the event team to make his part, as well as the entire experience, a super win. An hour with Tony often changes people's lives forever and impacts an organization's results immediately. He delivers value, a fun factor, and best practices people can really use.

Strategic Acceleration Facilitation Planning

Tony can do in a single day what takes many others days or even weeks to accomplish. He provides at your fingertips three decades of *Best*

RECALIBRATE

Practices, processes, and tools for accelerating dramatic, sustained results in any organization.

Collaborative Relationships

We selectively partner with organizations in a *Growth Partnership* arrangement. We supercharge and help winners win more. Most winning leaders know they can always win better and faster by teaming up with the right people, adding the right resources, and becoming clearer on their vision. Our foundational methodology of *Clarity, Focus, and Execution* is deployed in such a way that our partners get the right *RESULTS Faster*!

We built a multi-million-dollar think tank seven minutes from Dallas-Ft. Worth Airport called the RESULTS Center (www.resultscenter.co). It is the ultimate destination where teams synergize, powerful plans are built, and individuals become energized to compress their time to turn visions into reality—often in less time than believed possible.

The ultimate think tank: a powerful place for holding strategic clarity and planning meetings

WHAT WE CAN DO FOR YOU

We have over 30,000 contacts, three decades of proprietary-built tools, multiple investment options, a hand-selected team, and a thirty-year proven track record, all to be leveraged with the right partners. We bring energy (*Vibe*) to the table.

Please visit www.tonyjeary.com as well as www. tonyjearytheresultsguy.com, and then reach out to us at info@ tonyjeary.com to discuss what we can do for you.

MIKE MCDANIEL

Throughout the years, Mike has encouraged, empowered, and motivated companies through energetic and insightful keynote speaking engagements. By incorporating personal stories, business strategies, and practical application scenarios, Mike helps bridge the gap in communication and execution for both large and small organizations.